Selling Nails on the Beach

An Original Collection of Reiki Poems

By Michael Smith

Old Line Publishing, LLC

Copyright © 2006 by Michael Smith

All rights reserved. No part of this book may be reproduced or transmitted in any form or by any means, electronic or mechanical, including photocopying, recording, or by any information storage and retrieval system, without permission in writing from the publisher.

Published by Old Line Publishing, LLC, Hampstead, Maryland
www.oldlinepublishingllc.com

Printed in the United States of America

Looking For A Publisher?

We are always looking for people knowledgeable within their fields. If you feel that there is a real need for a book regarding your particular area of expertise, we encourage you to contact us.

Old Line Publishing, LLC
P.O. Box 624
Hampstead, MD 21074
Phone: 410-259-8295
Fax: 410-374-9881
Email: oldlinepublishing@adelphia.net
Website: www.oldlinepublishingllc.com

Table of Contents

1   This Book
2   My Book
     Society As That
3   The Movie
     Love Is

BEACH

5   Wind Chimes
     Shell
6   Driftwood
7   Surfing The Portholes
     Going To The Beach
8   Sandcastles
     Fishing For Thoughts
9   Bridges
10   Beach Flag
     Looking For Water
     Be Still
11   Shore Bound
     Riding On That
12   Surfing
13   Sun And Ocean
     Deep Peace
14   The Whale
     Valerie On The Shore
15   Waves
16   I Am The Beach
     Glue
17   Desert

18   Ocean
19   Sand
     My Favorite Song
20   Skate Boarding
21   Sunken Ship
     Boating

SENSES

22   Look Really
     Tears
23   See The Oneness
     Senses
24   Touch
     Seeing
25   Seeing Clearly
26   Sound
     Walking
27   Pain
     Visualize
     Balance
28   Silent Wisdom
     No Mind-Ever
29   Mind Clearing
     The Song Of The Day
     Happiness
30   Dreams
     Racing To Find Peace

SEARCHING

31   The Witches Of The North

32   Finding Love
     Nothing To Do
33   Control
     Perfection
34   Winners Give Up
     Teacher Hunting
35   Today
     Let Go
36   Where Is Peace
     Completion
37   Racing
     Your Future
38   Paths
39   Time To Let Go
     You Are An Awakening Of Light
40   Letting Go
     You Are It
41   Seeking
42   Looking For Peace
     One
43   Teaching
     Illusions Of Peace
     Stop
44   Standing On The Edge
     Changing
45   Lose The Illusion
     Illusions

Table of Contents

46 Reflections Of Love

46 Looking

NATURE

47 Grass

Weeping Willow

48 The Wind

That

49 The Chameleon

50 Reflections

Cutting Grass

51 Love As A Cloud

52 Groundhog Day

Frogs

53 Dogs And Cats

Starlight

Groundhog Day Again

54 You Are The Sky

Always

IMMERSING THE MIND

55 Immersed

Your Mind Is Love

56 This Silence Is You

57 No Thoughts Bring Love

Words And Advice

58 Stop Reading Your Story

Wisdom

59 Labels

Hanging Thoughts

WRITINGS FROM THE OTHER SIDE OF THE FENCE

60 Over Here

Sharing Nothing

61 Painting

62 It Is...

Beauty

63 One Day

Words

64 Alone

Quiet Words

65 No Room For Two

Meeting

66 Bliss Is

Windows

67 Thank You My Love

Traveling

68 Poetry to Truth

Falling In Love

69 Being Love

Life

70 Carpe Diem

Dancing Lovers

This Wonderful State Of Nothing To Love

71 All There Is.. Is Love

72 Dear Peace

Worry Not

73 Prayer

73 Radio

74 Doing

After Death Experience

Church Bells

75 Prayer And Meditation

Most Important Message

CHILDREN

76 Message For My Children

77 I Saw Him As A Wall

78 A Son

Mother

79 My Children

A Talk With Son

80 PB & J

Father

81 Happiness Is

Two Boys

82 Baseball Is Heaven

STORIES

83 The Princess And The Alligator

84 Picture There

85 Story Of A Girl

The Flower

86 The Servant And The Princess

Photo Credits

Front Cover, Atlantic Dunes, Ocean City, Maryland, by Craig Schenning

Page 2, Rolling Hills, Carroll County, Maryland, By Michael Smith

Page 3, Movie Tickets, by Michael Connors

Page 4, Atlantic Dunes, Ocean City, Maryland, by Craig Schenning

Page 5, Shells, by Jane Sawyer

Page 6, Evening Waves, Ocean City, Maryland, by Craig Schenning

Page 7, Beach Umbrella, Halkidiki, Greece, by Jim Munnelly

Page 9, Stone Bridge, Baltimore County, Maryland, by Michael Smith

Page 10 (top), Beach Flag, MJedford, New Jersey, by Diane Holiday

Page 10 (middle), Blue Ripples, Edinburgh, Scotland, by Scott Liddell

Page 12, Beachboards, Langebann, South Africa, by Jaques Theron

Page 14, Whale Breach, by Matthew Hull

Page 15, Ocean Pier, by Yevgeny Eriskin

Page 17, Living Desert Zoo, Carlsbad, New Mexico, by Michael Smith

Page 18, Retreating Waves, Ocean City, Maryland, by Craig Schenning

Page 19, Grains of Sand, Ocean City, Maryland, by Craig Schenning

Page 20, Skateboard, by Michael Smith

Page 22, Ramsey Canyon Creek, Arizona, by Dawn Turner

Page 24, Tiger, by Michael Smith

Page 25, The Canopy, Thurmont, Maryland, by Craig Schenning

Page 26, Carlsbad Caverns, Carlsbad, New Mexico, by Michael Smith

Page 28, Cave under Alcatraz, California, by Bob Kimball

Page 31, Spooky Moon, by Jim

Page 32, Beaver Dam, by J. Gracey Stinson

Page 33, Bald Eagle, Point Lookout, Maryland, by T

Page 34, Stone Wall, by Yevgeny Eriskin

Page 36, Down The Line, Trenton, Maryland, by Craig Schenning

Page 37, Small Creek, by Unknown Photographer

Page 38, Moors Valley Country Park, Dorset, UK, by Colin Woodcock

Page 41, High Desert, New Mexico, by Michael Smith

Page 44, Produce Stand, Carroll County, Maryland, by Michael Smith

Page 45, Rio Gorge, Taos, New Mexico, by Michael Smith

Page 46, Glasses and Book, by Andrea Church

Page 47, Weeping Willow, Australia, by Simon Jackson

Page 48, Wildflowers, New Mexico, by Michael Smith

Page 49, The Chameleon, by Rob Carpenter

Page 50, Beautiful Sunset, by Mary K. Baird

Page 51, The Horizon, New Mexico, by Michael Smith

Page 52, Turquoise Frog, by Kevin Connors

Page 54, Wildflower Garden, by Jane Sawyer

Page 56, The Candle, by Michael Connors

Page 58, Ancient Books of Medicine, by Clara Natoli

Page 59, Bench In Snow, by Matthew Hull

Page 61, Sidewalk Art, by Michael Smith

Page 62, Boats At Moor, by Clara Natoli

Page 63, Sunset, Tampa, Florida, czbrat

Page 64, Waves on a Sandy Seashore, by Clara Natoli

Page 65, Open Door, Chouen, Morocco, by Hanspeter Stauffer

Page 69, Summer Pond, Hampstead, Maryland, by Michael Smith

Page 71, Garage Window, Italy, by Alberto Bairati

Page 73, Garden Angel, Hampstead, Maryland, by Michael Smith

Page 76, Empty Swings, Bisbee, AZ, by Ben Turner

Page 77, Abby Ruins, Ireland, by Michael Connors

Page 78 (top), NCR Bridge, Monkton, Maryland, by Michael Smith

Page 78 (bottom), Winding Creek, Monkton, Maryland, by Michael Smith

Page 79, Lightning, by Robert Boutin

Page 80, Peanut Butter and Jelly, by Craig Schenning

Page 81, NCR Trail, Monkton, Maryland, by Michael Smith

Page 82, Baseball, by Michael Smith

Page 84, Yellow Rose, by Derek Lilly

Page 86, Castle at Carreg Cennen, South Wales, by Dean Jenkins

Back Cover, Michael Smith, by Tricia Smith

Dedication

This book is dedicated to my best friend in life, Tricia,
and my little teachers Valerie, Nick and Ben.

Forward

"These poems are your bridge to...to what you have been searching for in and as life. To what has kept you running from one goal to the next in hopes of finding the end to your race. To what you have been seeking directly or indirectly as you follow through your own trail.

These poems are made for everyone. Everyone qualifies to be the hidden messages within these words. Everyone qualifies to be these blessings. Everyone is these blessings.

It's now time to end your search and fall into what you have been seeking. It's time now to allow the bottom of life to drop out to reveal its beautiful depths. It's time to stop and know your Truth. A Truth that will end your searching and chasing. A Truth that will end your desires to fix and control life...your life and others. A Truth that will allow you to sit in the open doorway where life and peace are one.

Uncover what you have been searching for and realize something very important. That it does not matter, who, what, how, when or why you are. You will just know you are That...then you will grab your bucket, your sign and your folding chair and laugh and...go sell nails on the beach!"

Introduction

As a 40 year old ex-spiritual seeker, I have spent the last 20 years of my life exploring the meaning, value, and purpose of life. One day, something occurred that cleared all the chatter and fear from my mind. The peace and connection I was seeking, became me. My world, thoughts, past, and future all became one. I was at peace and at home with myself and everything. I suddenly realized I had been "a drop of water in the ocean, looking for water."

This incredible feeling of connection with life was so strong that I had to put it in words as a teaching to others. The results are these poems and their hidden messages that I have written for you.

This book is designed to bring your awareness from the mind and thoughts to your connection with Oneness. Similar to Reiki, Massage, Meditation, Prayer, Yoga, etc... these poems cleanse your mind and expand your awareness beyond your body. These poems make you feel free and alive. Any poem in the book can be chosen at random to invigorate your day. The book can also be read by chapter as a teaching to steer you toward its hidden messages and your freedom. I have capitalized words within the poems to bring your attention to the transparency and Oneness that each of these words represents.

Imagine sitting on the beach and along comes a teacher of wisdom to point your attention to something you have forgotten. He reminds you of your connection with the sea, your connection with the sand and wind and the freedom that you have always known. This book is that teacher and you are the beach. This book will awaken the silent connection between you and the world. You will see your thoughts, others, and life as a part of you and all fears and threats will be truly seen as illusions.

Hopefully, these poems will allow you to lose yourself in nature and life. You will become the things you read about. You will become the ocean, the wind and the surf. You will become free. This freedom will continue as your mind is awakened even after the book is closed. I hope your life will be impacted as you slowly unfold your true being. Just as these words excite you, so shall "Selling Nails on the Beach" reveal your true nature.

This Book

This book is my attempt
My attempt to bring me to you
The me that is...
The oneness of every raindrop
The ocean blue that runs into all
The open door that you are sitting in

This book is my hope
My hope is that you live as you are...Love
Stop the chasing what you are
Stop fearing life
Stop thinking
Stop thinking you are not It
My hope is that you truly see your Oneness
Know the ocean that you are
Live as your Ocean
My hope is that you look into the stars at
night in amazement and
look into others the same way
as it is you

This book is my bridge
To unveil Truth and Freedom
To end your illusion and fantasy
To bring you over the fence to Aliveness, to
Life, to who you are
God, Life, Freedom, Peace, That, Oneness
& Love
That is you......you know this

This book is my gift to you
To let you go and play

Life will unfold for you
Just watch and play
Don't worry ...let it unfold
To reveal Love in others
Keep silent and enjoy the show

These poems are my words
Describing my galaxy of Peace
Touching the mist of the Ocean
The raindrop of a storm
The ray of the sun
Just tasting part of it all
exposes all of its flavor
For you as you
Which is enough

Dive into each wave and ride it
To Aliveness and Freedom
as you dance in its swell
and lose the illusion
of you and become Life

These words are your Life
Symbols pointing to the unpointable
The emptiness and peace that makes up
everything

This Book (continued)

The clear glue that holds life
The free openness that is you
These words are That
You are That
Now read on to your wholeness
Read on to be

Read on to know
and sit in your Peace...
for you are Peace
You will find it here because
there is something for everyone
Everyone is this Peace unaware.

Society as That

All children crying tonight
Stop and be still
You are Love

All teenagers lost in fear
Stop and be Still
You are Peace

All Mothers praying for healing
Stop and be still
You are God

All fathers pushing to make it
Stop and be still
You are It

And all lost ones in thought
Stop and be very still
You are Truth

All nations fighting to be free
Stop and be still
You are already Freedom

Know This in Stillness
It is You.

My Book

My Book is my hands
Folded together they guide me to inner peace
Opening up they reveal the inner peace in all I see

Providing a crossing from this to That
Building a bridge and then destroying it
No in, no out

The Movie

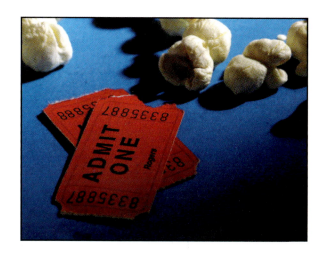

When the screen of life projects an illusion of fear
When the screen projects horror and misery
Look down at your popcorn box

Love Is

All there is ... is Love
Forms of Love... Love in form
There is no you.... There is no me

There is only Love
Love pretending to be us

Beach

The Ocean and the shore are your greatest teacher. Her silent words, sights, smell and touch reveals deep Freedom. Her soul is yours as yours is hers. Grab your chair and dissolve into your essence, the sun and wind await your remembrance.

Wind Chimes

Be like a wind chime
Flowing with the breeze in song

Many wind chimes are still in their boxes
Wrapped tight and secure
Knowing and being their price tag on the store shelf
Shiny, sparkly and new
Not knowing their true nature and freedom

Lose your price, let go of your box and leave the store
You are the wind also

Shell

A shell travels over time
Pushed, pulled and shifted
Across the bottom of the sea
Always knowing its true nature
Staying still while the sea moves
Its journey is polished to
reveal its new colors
Then it is passed up on the shore
Where its depths are realized
and becomes the beach

Driftwood

I was once driftwood
Drifting in the giant blue ocean
Trying to get to shore, trying to move
Drifting here and there in circles

One day the ocean spoke to me
"I am you also"
I felt her hug all around me
I suddenly began to move.. out, down, left, right
I was everywhere

Now I drift across along the earth
Holding the earth together
Kissing the shores and reflecting the sky
Offering my deep blue cool healing to All
as they drift into my path

Surfing the Portholes

That first endless ride on a board
Skating smoothly across in flight
A night of endless play in the summer
Magical excitement without time
The first kiss
To touch beauty and be Free
Sunrise on the beach
Seeing and Knowing Peace
Quietness after loss of a loved one
But feeling their presence as Stillness
The opening song of a concert
Bringing alive every cell of the body
Birth of child
Opening Love to the what is Known
Morning snowfall
Offering its natural quiet
unfolding as All
Loving smile of a stranger
Reaffirming Oneness
These are the portholes of Life to fall in
These are the portholes of Life to never come out of
Enjoy your fall and lose
yourself in it until you find your Self

Going to the Beach

Travel from here to there
Everything moves except Being
Scenery changes
Body changes
Experience changes
All are new forms of Being
Same me always on the beach
Same me Free as the waves
Being here once again
Knowing the quiet message of the Sea
"Love... we are all one" she whispers

Sandcastles

"Who" made the sandcastles?
They are all the same
Grains of sand, water and Silence
Soaking in the sun
Becoming the warm breeze

Digging deep into the Sand
We feel the Beloved
That oneness we are
Digging into our foundations and essence
That... turning grains of sand to beaches we are

Our sandcastles are the same
Makers are the same

Fishing for Thoughts

Like a fishhook thoughts can carry you away
Beyond the safe reef
Beyond the beautiful blue water where life abides
Be a fish and you get hooked
Be the Ocean and see the hook pass through
Hooking onto everything and nothing

Thoughts are puddles of water in the Sea
Part of it but trapped in illusion
Be your illusion, be the puddle and become the Sea

Bridges

God is over there
Love is over there
Peace is over there
Two words can bridge "you" to there
I am

I am the Wind
Walking through Wind
I am the wind

Seamless, flowing and moving as All
We brush through our Love
and race off together

Out to sea in the night, we merge into the stars
I am a wave
Moving through my Sea
Boundless, flowing and moving as All
Moving to shore I crash and become the beach for a moment
Then back again

I am this Moment
This Moment is always here
I am this Moment all around now
This Moment within and without me

Beach Flag

Like a flag in a summer day
Warm sun and breezes brush me
Snow and Ice tomorrow
Still the same flag
Still moving as life
Just as the ocean
reflects her sun and clouds
We change not in reflecting night and day
We are all flags
floating in the summer breeze
Unfolding to what is there
Unfolding to our Self

Looking For Water

One day I realized
I am a drop of water in the Ocean
Looking for water

Be Still

Stop, Be Still, and allow the clouds, the rain, the wind and sun...
Stop, Be Still, and allow the clouds, the rain, the wind and sun...
Love is All

Shore Bound

Surf rolls in and touches your feet
You are the same cool water on your toes
Salt air breezes by as you breath in
Your are the same breath and scent as before
Sun reflects on the water and shines in your eyes
Reflecting on life you are the same here now as always

Nothing changes only the shore
Shifting grains of sand to reveal new beaches
All the while remaining as That
Changing scenery each moment
All the while remaining as That

As you sit once again shore bound looking out at your Self
Shifting through life to reveal a new you
All the while remaining as That

Riding On That

As I surfed the wave
I saw the ocean
A Silent teacher whispers to remind me of Truth
The lapping of the waves touch my ankles.
Reminding me of the ocean I am.
My Seas move into the world in front of me
Opening the door to depths within Life
Allowing me to see more and lose myself
Only to gain the world through greeting my Self

Surfing

Bobbing in the sea there is no me
Silence speaks between each wave
The open sea pulls as we go out to One
Dissolving the movie of life leaving it behind to run on its own
I merge into That place I know
Sitting on the other side
No thoughts or time
Movement flows within sequence
Rising as the wave I am dancing as That
Held in balance, I am the glue of balance
Cutting through we race forward
Surfing the edge between illusion and Life
This place is just me always known always Free
We expand as Freedom and stretch across the Sea
Carving silently and smoothly becoming the open skies
Bigger, larger out into it all
Held up as the Truth
I become the waves moving and all directions become One
Right and wrong are now nothing as Freedom is Here

Sun & Ocean

The sun crosses the sea in this morning
You first see its rays of light touching the waves as it comes to you
You feel the warmth hit your face and clear your mind
You feel the warmth enter into your body and warm it from within.

You are the rays of light
The light, in the light.
Where do you think you have to go?

Deep Peace

You are the deep ocean
Calm and Peace

You are a splash of water rolling up to shore
With the Ocean as your Being

Aware of your deep peace
You splash onto the sand to play

In forgetting Fullness
Your Peace rolls in like the tides
Covering your being in deep blue Freedom and Love
Silently speaking to you as you
Reminding you that you are the Play, the Sand, the Shore

As everything reflecting in your waters is you also

The Whale

As the whale, I am the Sea
Diving deep into my Self
Surfacing to the top
Where all waves run and splash
Splashing in my depths we become One
Currents move through me
Leaving no effect
I am the current, the wave,
the whale, the Ocean
Moving in Peace

Valerie on the Shore

She is not Valerie
She is not a girl
She is not a mind or thought
Just light playing with itself
Skipping, running as her tide rolls in
Jumping , hopping as her sand is dug up
Leaving traces on her shore for a moment
That a dance is here to re-mind of One
Wind joins in and invites the sun to reveal the endless harmony
A joyous song plays

Waves

A wave catches the wind and gravity
    Looking for the ocean

A wave builds up in form
    Looking for the ocean

A wave rides to shore
    Looking for the ocean

A wave moves along with other waves
    Looking for the ocean

A wave peaks in vastness
    Looking for the ocean

A wave crashes on the shore
    Looking for the ocean

A wave settles into its natural tide
    As the ocean, it's always been

I am the Beach

I am the Beach
I am the sand, the heat, the dryness
A single grain of sand and the shoreline

The surf comes in
Reminding me I am the Ocean
That has always been

Covering my shores revealing and opening up depths
Just as suddenly the tide comes up it goes out
Coming and going is the tide
Moving to and from we play like the starfish

Glue

Pelicans soar in formation
Grass grows as millions of twins
Cars speed on the highway together

The suns rays touch equally
The waves of the ocean line up to crash
Rip tides keep the sea back
Grains of sand connect to form the beach

Conversation becomes a score of song
Relationships unfold as wildflowers

We are in control?

Desert

I have built the raft, and sail off
Leaving all paintings of life on shore

Drifting out to Sea, One am I
The sea, sky , sun and wind am I

A drink of loneliness and emptiness
A drink of aliveness
Quenches my thirst for further travel
Washes my mind and removes fear

I sit in this beauty
With nothing to say

But hear whispers of Peace filling my mind
Language becomes like a square wheel

Returning to shore
My paintings come alive with depth
So bright and vivid I dive into them
Bringing the Sea with me

Ocean

The salt within the air
The silence between waves crashing
The endless deep blue
The harmony of the wind and sun
Where these things join you are

The bird songs in the brush
Breezes and stillness dancing around
Shells holding a place in the surf
Where these things join you are

The setting sun paints the sky pink
Kites fly high into the air
Children laughter adding sweetness to the air
Time and purpose paddle out
Where these things appear you are

You are this mixing and birth place
You are this... Free
You are ..... breath of Life

Sand

Every grain of sand stands alone
Together they make a beach
Within each is That
Aliveness, Silence, You
Holding the universe together

Beach and water appear separate
Yet both harmonize to become the shore
Water carries sand as sand carries water
Back and forth their playing is the glue

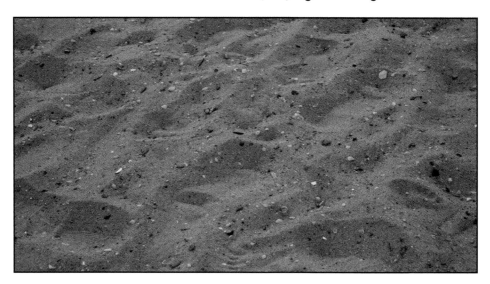

My Favorite Song

Is Everything
The sound of the day
Waves crashing
Birds song in the distance
Humming of machines
Distant voices in song

A chorus with an invisible score
Grand dynamics and moving pauses
Blending together to encase my existence and wash it away

Skateboarding

Floating and Flying
Moving free
Across and lifted
Each place is me

No future or past
To make me forget
Life as I am
In a stage that is set

It brings me here
This place of fun
No aging or worries
Immediate and now
As the rays of the sun

Smiling inside as I go in the open door
Carving through life
Leaning into everything to explore
Each turn and lean becomes me
Expanding to be Free
Stretching out my Self
Simply to Be

Sunken Ship

"Drop anchor" yells the captain
We have sunk to the bottom
Lock us in this place we know
Where all ships search but few find

The door was in the rubbish
As we crashed into it, breaking it
It was open all along
and devoured our world into it

Now there is no door, no there
Only here, deep within everything

So, hold on drop anchor and lock us in
Our ghosts are dancing on the roof

Tapping away trying to bring us up
We dance with them anyway
As old songs reveal newness

Boating

Speed boats run through and bounce over all the waves
Pushing through life searching
Their wake creates more waves for other boats to hop over
The ride is fun but the speeding gets tiring
The search continues

Be the tanker sunk at the bottom of the Ocean
She sits in stillness aware of all the speed boats
Aware of all the waves
She is the Waves
She is the Ocean
She is the Stillness
Silent in the depths of Peace
Searching no more
As she sits in golden treasure

Senses

These poems will guide you and bring you into That. Look, feel, and notice what lies between your senses. What lies between the touch? Who is seeing? Who is listening? Where does the speaking come from? Your senses are both the beginning and ending to the ring.

Look Really

See a simple tree
Know the silent clear light that is life within the tree?
That is you
Look at your neighbor
See the silent clear light that is life
It speaks to you
"we are it"
Even during conversation another language is spoken
A dance takes place without music

Tears

Your tears are the river

The silent river of Life that is All

Follow this river to its Source

Where tears begin

And find ....Love

See The Oneness

Don't live in separation
The Love you are
Is All
Your strangers
All cry silently within
As they are still children
Weeping in the dark
Believing in an illusion of darkness
Be with them
For their tears are Yours

Senses

Sound is like a stream of Peace flowing
Taste is a rainbow just forming in the dew
Touch is the expressed experience of Love
Smell is bringing into your being a moment as All
Sight is staring at your Self in forms of stillness

Be the place where one sense ends and another begins
Be the place between seeing and hearing
Be the place between feeling and smelling

Be the place where all the senses join
This is the senseless place where all is One.

Touch

Stillness is always here
A touch brings opens you to it
Changing you to Stillness
Like a drop of water into the Sea
Floating into home and richness
Quenching thirst forever

Touch stillness
Change scenery to background
Allowing thoughts to pass over
Touch is a key to unlock the open door...
to Home

Seeing

See what can't be seen
It is within each sight
A rainbow of options
Deep and wide into the illusion that plays out

A monkey will follow the illusion and try to play in it
A donkey will carry the illusion
A shark will attack the illusion hoping to find Truth
An eagle will fly across the illusion and not see what holds it up
But the Tiger sees Truth
A Tiger will see a monkey following nothing
A donkey carrying itself
An eagle flying no where
And a shark will kill everything like a fool thinking that a fish can die of drowning.

A fire cannot bring more light by setting fire to fire.
Be the Tiger and see IT as you knock from the inside of the door

Seeing Clearly

Look for a new color, a new color that is you
This color has been here your whole life
You have been looking at it and looking for it in your search
This color is the color that runs through everything and is everything
Once you see this new color you will see your Self
You will see the canvas that life is painted on

Look at these words
Look in between these words and your nose
Look and see this new color it is the color Clear
Its invisible yet visible and its everywhere
Look around

The clear color is the canvas of life
It runs through all
Close your eyes and see it
Open your eyes and see it everywhere

You are the silent and radiant color clear
You are That
See you are That as you clear your mind
See how That is connected to everyone and everything
You cannot, not be That - is it clear now?

You are the tiny space between the pencil and paper
You are the space within the ink of these words
You are these words
You are Love, In Love, All Love, Love Expressing

Sound

Listen to this moment
To the sounds of the day
These sounds come from far and near all to you
As you also go far and near to the sound

Listen for a special sound
It is the sound of nothing.
It is the sound of space
It is the sound of space between a sound
It may just be a millisecond but it's there

All sound is created from nothing
As a note is played within the note is nothing
Every sound is space vibrating
Such as you are space vibrating

Nothing can be heard in everything
Allow yourself to listen now to the Silence
This Silence is you

Allow your Self to expand to the silence, become the silence
All sounds are extensions of you expanding
All sounds you hear should remind you of how endless You are

Walking

Walk in Peace and walk anywhere
Walk in Peace and be everywhere
Walk in Peace and all will know you
Walk in Peace and music will play
Walk in Peace and need nothing

Pain

Echo of pain goes on forever
Where it starts and goes to am I

Like a bell ringing in the town
Become the ring
Then echo and fly out to nothing
Where you stop is who you are.

As a cloud stretches across the sky
Thick at first but then breaking up
Spaces of sky peek through as it thins out
Your spaces within pain is your sky peering through
Reminding you of your deep blue vastness

Visualize

Dreaming in deep sleep Who am I?
Sitting watching the sunrise in silence, Who am I?
Riding my bike across the long highway, Who am I?
Holding my baby and rocking into sleep, Who am I?
Everything expanding in stillness and Love, can there be more?

Balance

I used to live as I
Balancing between spirit, body and I
Like a frog landing on lily pads
I would hop into the body
Hop into the spirit
Hop into I
Now I am Spirit
Floating in All

Silent Wisdom

The quiet knowing of your real truth
Can be felt in others
Passing by in thoughts, sleeping
Awake you know their presence

Just as the birds know to fly south
And the bear knows to hibernate
That which moves them is you also
Invisible but known
Deep and alive

The depths of That become the depths of me
Opening its doors to bring me in
To see the canyon of Peace that I am

No Mind - Ever

No thoughts - just God
No mind - just That
No one driving - just peace
Lift away your thought cloud
Its just you, clear passing thoughts
See your mind for what it is
An illusion
There is no mind
Just life
Life from the ground to the sky you are
From the east to the west you are
Life you are

Mind Clearing

You are That
The clear space all around, through and in you
You are endless, open and forever

Breath deep and let go...all is cared for
Know that you, the air, the sky are one...expanding
You are as far as you can think

You are silence, peace and love that permeates through all

You are the All

The Song of The Day

The song of the day is sung quietly
As the glue holding sound together
Its notes are distant within the noise of the city
When all are sleeping and dreaming their life
I find my Self awake listening to their chorus sing a beautiful song together
Unaware of their silent performance they sing in Love
As I sit within their song of the day

Happiness

Happiness is the gentle state of Peace
This state of Peace can be found in everything
From the Pachelbel to the jackhammer

Don't chase happiness
You will never catch it
Stop and feel it, its right Here its You

Dreams

You are Free... in your dreams (and all of life)
No wanting, no wishing, no time, just You
Happy, laughing, and playing

In your dreams feel the comfort, why is it there?
You are surrounded by love
Surrounded by family
You are Home
Home in your land, feeling warm, feeling safe, being Love

You are your dreams
A cup of drink passing from day dreams to night
The cup is there in both
All visions day and night contain the same cup
Paint all dreams clear and the cup remains

Racing to Find Peace

On you mark, get set, go
The race to find peace is on
Off they go looking everywhere
Collecting, buying, and chasing
What they already have and are...
Peace

On your mark, get set, go
I just sit and open my eyes
No where to go
Nothing to collect
I am Peace
I win the race
I lose the race
I am the race

Searching

The search will always continue as long as you keep thinking that something better is the answer. As long as you think better is someplace else it will be. These poems will point to the place that keeps moving along with you in your search, thus revealing to you that you have always been standing on the finish line.

The Witches of the North

Searching, Exploring, Dreaming
With their buckets full of spirit
Filling them up
Passing them around for drink

The witches of the north are imprisoned in their stew
Cooking, cooking, cooking
The more they cook, the more their customers eat
Cooking buckets and pots of the latest stew
Never filling their search, they continue cooking
Unaware that their meal is already complete and their customers full

Finding Love

To find God.....do nothing
You are then God doing nothing
To find Peace.....breath deeply
You are then Peace breathing deeply
To find Love...touch your heart
You are then Love touching your heart
To find Truth.....look at others
You are then Truth looking at itself

Nothing to Do

There is nothing you have to do
The Mystery will move you to do it
Just as the robin suddenly builds her nest
Just as the beaver suddenly builds his damn
Mystery will move you
Thoughts and mind are not
Like the robin you ride on the back of Mystery
Like Buddha, Jesus and a newborn baby
Mystery dissolves you into her soup

Control

Bugs fly
Oceans bring tides
Forests change color
Thoughts appear

Eagles soar
Salmon swim
Light reflects off the waves
Thoughts take a place

Bears hibernate
Children fall into sleep
Light dissolves and stars appear
Thoughts go where?

Perfection

Names and reputations burn out like embers
Turning to dust in the night
Building and holding up a name
Watch others to see how you should look, talk and live
Judge your self according to media, and casual opinion
Work on ourselves spiritually to ensure a future happiness for our self
Walk through life with walls and fences up at all times to protect your self from invasion of pain and hurt.

All this work is useless like a gardener watering orchids in the swamp

Your Truth cannot be improved, only discovered by stopping

Winners Give Up

To end the race and win
You must die into Truth
The thinking life is a maze of walls
After you are done and can't climb any more walls
Give up
Fall and rest into your Self
And see your walls
They are made of Peace also

Teacher Hunting

Looking for a teacher?
Words of wisdom
Reflections of truth

Look no further
Your teacher is

Is.... people
Brother, mother, friend, stranger
Rivers, flowers, oceans, trees and sky

Your teacher is a bread truck passing by
Leaving a scent of fresh bread
Providing a deeper presence after they pass

Today

Today I chose to look for Love
The more I looked the more I found

The changing world full of fear is but a dream
The purpose of the dream is the awakening

Awaken to what is always there
Your Self
Love
The Background

Always there is what is searched for by the seeker
Looking outward at movie
When the screen is Life

Let Go

Let go and you lose:

Your false illusion
You lose ...your thoughts of need to do
Your fears of death and loss
Your responsibility for making it happen
Your worries
Your time
Your identity
Your loneliness
Your pain
Let go and you loose.... all of this
Let go and you gain
Nothing and everything

Where is Peace?

There are no doors to peace.
Peace is not some place
Peace is not a goal or ending
Its here and it is you

It is the background and foreground of your days
It's the days itself

Don't get lost in thought
Don't get lost in future or past
Future and past you are

Look to see if "you" exist
Peace you are... not a "you"
No in, no out

Completion

Life is never complete
Life is never ending
Life is never done creating itself
You are never done creating life
Because you are Life
Existing, growing, changing always

Racing

Life is a race...
Yet, the finish line keeps moving
The faster you go the more you miss
What is missed is Nothing

Your Future

Does the river declare its path?
A storm decide its fury?
An oak tree chose its size?
Do you chose your height, skin color?

Look for a separate person in life and find trouble
Look for ways to satisfy your dreams and meet fear
Look for solutions to past pain and relive drama

The open window showing all this has the answer
As the window itself is showing the scene and is the scene
You are the window too
Becoming the wind that flows though
Becoming the moonlight that glows
The sounds of the earth reaching

Paths

You can be diminished
You can be bruised
You can be battered
You can be treated like a child
You can be embarrassed
You can be damned

True all of this does happen to you - and its fear
But you are not this

Deep inside is the true You
and You are

The Silent peace under a birds wing in flight
The soft tide rolling in around the world now
The quiet space between the breaths of all new born children
The Silent forming of dew on the morning grass
The clear knowing of That between your thoughts
The ever expanding sky

You are the river of all of these things flowing and unfolding
These things are you
Remember That

Time to Let Go

Let go, relax, rest your head on this pillow.
Just for this moment do nothing

Become this silence and space

Listen to the subtle silence within everything

That silence is you
You are...... Being
You are....... Peace
You are........ Love
You are........ Joy

Feel your Self go out to all sound
Sit, be the stillness.... rest
You are All

You Are - An Awakening of Light

The fat man will consume all the money in search of Truth
Drink all the wine to forget
Carve a single path in the woods only for he

The skinny man will save and give to needy
Drink wine to entertain
Carve paths for everyone to follow

The odd search for awakening is painted by all
Colors of light and pale
All artists paint the canvas unaware that
They are the painting, the brushing, the dying of the canvas

Letting Go

When you let go... you let grow
Its finally time to let go of all the things you feel you have to do.
Let go of all your worries.
Let go of all you feel you are holding up
It will be OK - you know That
Let It unfold naturally, the way you unfolded and came into this world
It was natural, no help from the mind
Rest into That which you are made of
Love, Peace , Silence, Clarity
You know This, you feel This at times but continue to struggle in pain
It is time now to walk, listen and be different.
Let go of the drama, it will still be there but not within you.
Become That, follow me and watch the drama not live it
Peace is within you
Peace is You

You are It

You are it
Look no further

Seeking just brings separation
Separating you from it
Rest into what you are.... It
It's that simple

Feel That within you
Look for That in everyone
Listen for That now in all sound as all
sound
Breath That
All thoughts are That

Now get rid of the "you" and feel Peace
Now "you" are ...."In Love"
You are Love

Go play - all thoughts are just clear and
ride on the surface transparently

All thoughts are Love also
All that is touched, seen and heard is You...
is Love

There is no goal, no finish line, Love is all
You are All

Seeking

What you seek you are
Seeking Peace, you are Peace
Seeking Love, you are Love
Seeking to fill that void, you are the void

Rest into That
That is what you are
All is That
There is nothing else but That

Love within is you
Love is in and out, there is no escaping it
Because...you are It.

Now look deeply for you
Drop the you and become Life.

Looking for Peace

As you look for Peace in your life
Don't look for it in others
They are just mirrors of you

Don't look for it in solitude
That is just your mind quieting

Don't look for it in texts
That is just whisperings to keep you focused

Don't look for it in nature
It can't bee seen there either

Peace can only be found in one place
Everywhere - Looking is ineffective

One

Looking for the One is impossible
One is everywhere
One can't be found here, cause then One is not there
One can't not be there if One is here
Trying to look for One is similar to looking for clouds in the fog
One will grab your ankles and drop you into her depths
Lie you on the ground to see the river
The river of Stillness that goes out
One will keep opening up open doors
Exposing the rooms of the house
Clearing the walls that limit you
By allowing you to see they are Nothing
One will make you feel Alive and not you
Limitations and separateness will drop
So will right and wrong as life opens up for play

Teaching

No Teacher
Nothing to learn
No book to read
No lecture to hear
Just Silence
The golden teacher
A place to rest
A place to be
This teacher is everywhere
Just a thought away
That comes from Silence
As does all

Illusions of Peace

Like a storm coming into the valley
Mind and thoughts sit on Peace
Clashing and rumbling to bring attention
Just as storm clouds pass by
So do thoughts
With bellies full, but empty
Full of sound and silence within
Your storms remind you of your Peace
Your storms are Peace showing up in new
ways
Don't fall for their disguise
Underneath the masks is the Beloved
Underneath the mask is You.

Stop

What are you afraid of
Don't keep running and searching
Don't be afraid to Stop and see
At first you will see madness and chaos
You will see the waves you have created
You will see the ripples of your mind
Stop, let it settle
See Now
See the Truth in the ripples
Who really made them
Why are they all the same
Made of the same Stuff
Made of the un manifested
Made of the same Essence as you
Sit in your own ripple
Feel it wash away you
Wash away till there is Nothing
Then you have found your Self

Standing on The Edge
(A Surfer's Poem)

Deciding to go or not
I suddenly see the edge as the go
The point to stand and lose your legs
No need for them anymore
There is not any more forward to go
Like a surfer or skater riding the tip
All is behind him, within him
Free flowing all moves in flight
Held up to soar by That
With arms stretched out
Sun, reflections on the water and breezes
The wings of heavens open up to carry all
illusions and fears into Aliveness
Stepping into the open window
The board rider loses himself as Freedom
Riding the edge where That sits waiting
Waiting to be joined, That is in progress
Bringing Life into Being
Standing on the edge is the last stance
A lifelong existence that we are
With all here and not here at the same time
The place to ride Free

Changing

You are better off trying to change the taste of an apple
Then trying to change the behavior of another
The film is running and the picture is projecting
What comes cannot be touched or moved
It moves in its own way through its own time
Revealing its gifts
In your movement you are drops of rain moving into a puddle

Lose the Illusion

Its not there
Its not later
Its not earlier
Its not going to be a way
Feel a way
Become a way
Its simple - You

Illusions

Even though Nothing is eternal
The illusions are fun.
What would it be without illusions, deep space
Even boring would be something.
So I enjoy all my illusions
An illusion in an illusion as I watch them pass by
as I become them
All passing by as me

Reflections of Love

You are a reflection of Love
Every set of eyes you see reflects your love
Look into the world and see your beauty
Look into the sky and see your stars
Look into the ocean and see your depth

You are a reflection of Love
Look into your heart and reflect its magic
Look into strangers and lighten their hopes
Look into misery and reflect freedom
Look into pain and reflect healing

You are a reflection of Love
Passing Love to all you see
All you see is a reflection of your Self

Looking

I was a teacher
I was looking for my eyeglasses
I was wearing my eyeglasses

One day I found them on my nose
Then I began to see the World

Nature

We are brought back to who we are again and again through something that we can't see, touch or capture..... Nature

Grass

Blades of grass are you!
Bowing and locking yourself
together in Silence
As God, Galaxy and Truth
never make you, never destroy you
Growing together as the One

Weeping Willow

Young and small
I feared the weeping willow tree
An illusion of giant arms grabbing me as
I tugged on her branches
Looking back I see through this illusion
As the deep ocean under her waves
I now tug her branches
And the weeping willow comes to help
Her arms are mine as we hug

The Wind

I was once the wind
Pushing trees and gently plucking their leaves off
I was once the wind
Tearing through windows brushing across human faces
I was once the wind

Now I am human, as I feel the cold wind seep into my body
I was once the wind giving breath to life
Now I breath in the wind of life

That

Like a flower pushing through the earth
Love directs and carries Beauty
Through all its phases
Never leaving
Always there
For simple Beauty

The Chameleon

Like the chameleon, blend to what is
In rain become wet
In snow become cold
In sun become warm
In nature become silent
In family become a caregiver
In sports become courageous
In a crowd become the noise
In silence become still
In Peace become content
In nothingness lose the you and blend into space

Now don't limit yourself like the chameleon to what is
Become all of it at once
As you are all of it
The rain, snow, sun and wind
Blowing across your faces in a crowd
Riding as the sound of the echo fading into your Self
All at once it is you, all at once THAT

Reflections

Clouds move, become that shadow
Cooling the earth, become the cooling

Wind blows, become the wind
Chimes sing, become the ringing
Rain falls, become each droplet
Rivers form and we are guided to sea
All stops and become the Stillness

Like the chameleon reflects color
Become what is
Changing to the Now
Noise, Silence, Drama, Love
All passing to us
All us

Cutting Grass

Cutting grass
Just That
No thoughts
No me
No judgments
Just That moving now
Simple, Free
I am work
I am doing
I am Life

Love as a Cloud

Extend your arm and reach out your hand
Now close your hand
You just grabbed the sky
Its all around you
Within you
It is you

As a cloud thinks it is separate from the sky
It plays, floats and looks separate
But is One with the sky always

You are like the cloud
Thinking you are separate is just a game
Like children playing brother and sister
Children playing parent and child
You are playing
Now wake up to your birth nature - Love - its you

Groundhog Day

Each day is the same
Just the scenery changes
We all play on the same Stage
Create on the same Canvas
Write on the same Paper
Feel the Love that we are
There is no change

Frogs

Maybe the frogs have it right
Sitting still, nothing to chase, nothing to buy
Rain is their friend, rain is them
Watching us rush in madness gathering stuff
Stuff that will allow us to one day rest
Like a frog

Stop like the frog, allow it to move
Day will come and night will follow
All with no effort from you
What is your job? Enjoyment!
Take your seat and enjoy the show
You are a frog watching yourself dance on the stage

Dogs and Cats

A dog and a cat go to the movies
The dog barks all through the show at each picture
The cat silently stares at the fly on the screen

Star Light

A starlight shines in the night
What is at the beginning of the starlight
What is That, that creates the light
Invisible, silent pulsation's
expanding everywhere
That is You.

Groundhog Day Again

Every Day is like groundhog day
"It" is always the same
Only the scenery changes
Weather, people, thoughts, events
Pass by like a parade
All new always changing and growing
All made up of the same stuff - Love
So the Groundhog appears just for the fun
He too sees his shadow and laughs at the illusion
Knowing he is the Shadow

You are the Sky

You are the sky
Being a cloud, bird and sun

You re the ocean
Being a wave, a fish, sand and rocks

You are human pretending to be not
All that is

Always

Just as a flower is always in nature
And the earth is always in space
You are always in Love

Love cannot be lost or left

Every movement, sound, emotion comes from
And is Love..... Is you.

Immersing The Mind

Improve, control, tune up and stilling the mind. These are all the tricks we are learning. Instead of teaching tricks to the mind lets include it in Life. Dissolve and immerse the mind into what it is... Life. Don't see the mind as a wall to your salvation. See it as you see the wall, an open door to All.

Immersed

I have dissolved into the Beloved
I knock and wait for others to enter
But they are all still dancing in the play
Running in the scene or drowning in their waves
I wait Immersed unable to explain

Your Mind is Love

Thoughts are just Light and Love
All that is the same as you
You are Light and Love
You are the clear never ending stream of Love
Silently running throughout the galaxy.
You are Silence everywhere
You are Love everywhere
See how this works. Now your mind is Love too.
In fact there is no mind, there is no you,
There is just Love, playing with Love.
Expand your thoughts out into nothing
Your thoughts become clear and nothing
Thoughts just trickle in silently if at all
As you rest in Love

This Silence is you

You are all silence
All peace
All space
All sound
All breath
All thoughts
You are No thing No where Now

Feel your Self as clear
Feel the clear run all through you
Dissolve into the clear
Dissolve the you into That clear
Now walk through your clear world

Thoughts, words, others are all you
Clear images and sounds coming from nothing, being nothing and returning to nothing.
All life is the dance of expression.

No Thoughts Bring Love

Don't live your life in fantasy
Going in that direction is very hard
It's the long way from the Source
It is like a mule dragging his load over the mountain
Go into the mountain
Become the mountain
And the load will lighten
Don't try to get to Truth through the mind
Discussing and bartering points is useless
It just leads to more bartering
Mind will dissolve when Truth shines
Shine Truth by facing eye to eye
Witness the Silence within your partner
Be the Silence
Hold and be the Source of the relationship
Let everything else grow as coming from That source

Words and Advice

Words and advice as useless as
Shining a glazed vase
Children are Peace already
Throw them on the pottery wheel
Let them spin and laugh
In silent sleep little faces of Peace
They know their Truth
Don't take that away from them
Like a potter burnishing a vase
Be the bagwal to the kiln
The protective wall of Truth
By resting within their Essence

Stop Reading Your Story

Mind brings you to many places
There are great chapters in "your book"
Be the Reader of the book not the book
As the Reader, see the transparency of the story
It shapes and molds to character not the Reader
Be the Reader and close the book of stories
These stories are the bricks to your walls
To bring you back to the Reader

Wisdom

That voice within all
With a thousand angles to show us
With a million ways to feel its depth
Always the teacher to remind us
Remind us of who we are and how deep we go
Wisdom plays a subtle song within all our meetings
Allowing us to see the purpose of our meeting
To see the canvas from the painting
The pause from the note
Wisdom is the thousand page book that opens up with
Each grain of sand
Revealing its lessons that we already know.

Labels

Remember do not let your mind label you today
Its all just energy named and evaluated by the mind
You are the namer naming itself

Hanging Thoughts

Images of the future
Things to do, get and see
Ways to feel and days of the week
Hang in my mind
Where do these images hang from
Where does their hook lie
Images hang on me
Emptiness and Aliveness
I remove the hook from the thought
as it lays on my body and becomes empty and Free like me

Writings From the Other Side of the Fence

What once was simple faith and knowledge, A peak or look at what is on the other side
One day became the other side, Now the story is told from the Within
Life is lived as the Within, Yet the fence is not there anymore to separate
The fence to the playground now surrounds everything
Everything is now inside, The within is the without

Over Here

Over here my mind is clear
The ceiling of thought has opened up
There is no barrier to heaven
I am Love and extend straight up and out to everything
To the left and right is Love and Peace disguised as people and objects

I close my eyes and become Love
Melting and dissolving into All
With eyes open I see Love
I am all Love, so is everything else
There is no more me just Love singing and dancing to Love

Sharing Nothing

I shared my Love with a friend
We both were That, nothing but That
We talked about Nothing
How great is Nothing
Felt the Love of nothing
Shared a moment of Nothing and everything.

Painting

I paint my world piece by piece
Each day painting Love
Brushing over old images with new color

First I painted my portrait, Who am I
Next I painted the world as my portrait

This painting never began
It never ends

As I am the picture, the painting, the color, the brush and the audience

It is....

It is timeless
It is not good
It is not bad
It is beyond good and bad
It is me
It is you
It is everywhere
It is alive
It is Love
It is Peace
It is Silence
It is US
You are Peace dreaming that you are not Peace but looking for Peace.

Beauty

Speed boats move to fast to notice Beauty
They speed from one place to another
Looking, searching, screaming their engines
The more they go the further they are from Beauty

Today I tried to show a speed boat Beauty
All I received was a confused look that informed me

Beauty is the speed boat riding on looking for Beauty

62

One Day

One day you are looking at life saying that is real
The next day you are looking at life saying That is real

Words

Words cannot describe
The ocean and the sky joining as one
Wrapping around and within me
As we soar through the heavens

Words cannot describe
Being the silent stream of thought
That floats above transparently
Becoming the river of Peace

Words cannot describe
This secret love
That makes the best music, food, dance and laughter
Simple toys bobbing in the Ocean

Alone

I am All
All is me
I am thus alone

Quiet Words

Quiet words are spoken everywhere
Words of Love
Words of Laughter
Words of Peace
Words that whisper always in your heart
Quiet words are the trees
Quiet words are the grass
Quiet words speak within our words
They sing within our songs
Quiet words are That

You must be quiet to hear them, they are silent
You must be Here to hear them they are strong
As they hold us together

Like gravity pulling in the tide
We are pulled on shore to break and open
Open to hear quiet words

No Room for Two

My house is very large
its rooms extend forever
its windows are open always
Yet only One can enter the open door
There is no room for two

Meeting

I meet my Self in others
But others don't see it
Their Aliveness covered in thought
Those I meet speak two languages
One language of the mind and one of silence
The latter required no words but carrier of our Self
Molding our words and allowing us to sit in silence
No words spoken but plenty known
Nothing has to be accomplished in the meeting

Bliss is

Bliss is There
Like the non blowing breeze
Its the place you fall into at night
As you go to sleep
Falling into Truth
Falling into You

Fall into Bliss now
Become Silence
It required nothing, just noticing
The glue that holds the days scenery together..... is you
The freedom from thoughts and worries..... is you
The invisible depth known in everything....... is you
Peace... is you
Fall into it...
Nothing is required

Windows

I looked out the window at the world
I am safe here with the world there
The window protects me from coldness
I sit in peace alone

I now look out the open window as the world
I am safe, I am All, the world is Here
Each image an expression of me
Flowing, dancing, moving as Love
I sit and watch One

Even if your window is closed
Know that you can never shut it
What lies on the other side is you
You are the window, the shutting and Life

Thank You my Love

Thank you for bringing me there
That place not found in words
That place with no signs or directions
You opened up the open door and allowed me to see
See what was always there within

Thank you my love for leading the way
To my Truth
Re-minding me of my resting place
Which has been here all along

Thank you my love for being my teacher
Teaching me this Presence
and shadowing me all along my discovery

Thank you my love as we become closer beyond it as It.

Traveling

We think we are going somewhere
Moving from here to there

Like a video racing game only the scenery moves
Start your engines, hit the gas and bring on the scene
Bring it faster, slower to the left and right its all you

Like the salmon swimming in place against the river
All appears for the joy of seeing our Self
And we end up in the same place
Because we never left.

Poetry to Truth

I am not a good person
I am in need of help
I am scared of life
I have been hurt so bad
My body hurts
I need to be closer to Love
I want more Love
I like the Love I feel

I feel Love
I Am experiencing lots of Love
I am Love
Loves dissolves I
Just Love now
Love experiencing Love
Love is
Love is......me!

Falling in Love

You are Love
You are Love walking through Love
You are Love seeing Love
You are Love working in Love
You are Love sitting quietly in Love
You are Love thinking Love
You are Love listening to Love
You are Love breathing Love
You are Love! there is not You
Just Love experiencing more Love

Rest in your Self - Love
There is nothing you have to do
The subtle Silence
The Peace under the stars at night
The Quiet wisp under a birds' wings in
flight
Is all you

You are Love
The silent pull that drags the tide in
The space between the stars
The transparent stream that flows
and makes life dance
Is all you

You know this, you are This
You are This everywhere

You are Love
The silent connection between two strangers
The expanding sky reflecting the blue water
You are the reflection itself
The words on this page as they touch you
deeply
You are That depth
That Love
You are all that is Silent and Creating

Being Love

I Love
I Am Love
I am in Love
I am in total Love
I am in total happy Love
I am in total happy youthful Love
I am in total happy youthful passionate Love
I am in total happy youthful passionate Love for the moment

I am in total happy youthful passionate Love for the moment
I am in total happy youthful passionate Love
I am in total happy youthful Love
I am in total Love
I am in Love
I am Love
I Love
Being Love

Life

Life is...
The never ending space
that an echo fades to
You are That
Life drifting and
settling all around
Into the background
within everything
Rest as Life
All is you

Carpe Diem

Be the day
Seize That
That is the Day
Seize the Day
Seize That by Knowing there is Nothing to seize

Dancing Lovers

Your source is Love
It flows constant
Unnamed and silently
Speaking quiet words
To bring you Home

Love merging with Love
That is the dance of lovers
They dance not to end
They dance just to dance
With no purpose, no thoughts
Sharing the Self as One

This Wonderful State of Nothing to Love

Flickers of Light run through my window
Bringing my awareness to my Self
Like a bell ringing through the town
The Beloved calls me and reminds me
How vast is the Self
Echoing out to All as All

All There is... is Love

All there is.... is Love
Forms of Love - Love as form
There is no you
There is no me
There is only Love - Love is All
You and I are Love

Love knocks on my window inviting me to stay in
I for a long time have been leaving to go look for love
Tonight Love has locked the window to keep me Here
Here is where Love is
Here in Peace
Here in Clarity
Here in Freedom
Love then breaks the window to end the search
Inviting the out in and the in out
Love is neither in or out, It is both
I fall in Love and know I never fell out of Love

Dear Peace

Your words are whispered but always there
Your presence is felt but I am unaware
Your power spreads far beyond what I see
But know its there and alive as me

My hands move to the rhythm of the song you play
In time I am the orchestra knowing yesterday and today

Dear Peace I knew you once as a goal in my mind
Now I am you

Signed, Peace

Worry Not

Everything is already done.
The movie is already written.
You are just the drop of water on the salmons back swimming in the river
All that passes you
Is you going toward itself

Don't worry, your next thought is not made by you
It comes from Life
It goes to Life
You are That space which the thought lands and dissolves

When a flower blooms its petals, does it say "look what I did"? no.
Its nature moving through nature. So it is with you.

Prayer

Pray not for a way
Pray not to be open
Pray not for healing
Pray not for fortunes
Pray not even for love
Praying for something is like the sun requesting light
Or a lemon seeking to be sour
Pray as celebration in being the unawakened Truth in All

Radio

Life played in AM radio
Then I walked in the open door
Life plays in FM radio
Same songs, same sounds
More depth, just..... more

Doing

Everything we have ever done is connected
But never see the silent wisdom passed on
A bit of nothing that sits within all we do
that will carry me in Life

After Death Experience

I once died
Scattered across the dead land
I ran looking for the light
Not knowing my own shadow was me
I was the shadow that cast all light
Woven through everything as darkness
As I stared into the light searching, looking, waiting
Struggling, running, bleeding
I gave up the chase and scattered once more
Across the dead land
To rest in peace
It was then I saw darkness within the light
And I my Self within the darkness
Silence within the noise
Love within the violence
Heart within the body
Truth within the lies
The death of me dissolved into That

Church Bells

The hammer hits the bell, I awaken
The echo rings and I am Truth within this cavern of sound
The sound fades, I am still there
Echoing as silence as before awakening

Prayer and Meditation

Open the door we ask in prayer
Bring me there we ask in meditation
Help this person we ask in prayer
Let me hear you we ask in meditation
Bring silence we ask in prayer

We pray and meditate in trust
Of the silent voice that speaks Truth

When all the music stops and the play ends
Or all the music becomes loud and the play bloody
The silent voice becomes the wave to carry us
On this wave we realize we are the silent voice

Then the one door opens once
From That side revealing no sides
As we float out into All
Flooding the world In Love

We then pray and weep silently at the beauty
We then meditate and soar like an echo in a canyon

Each person we meet is cloaked In Love
Each function we do reveals us

Most Important Message

Nothing is.... Forever
Nothing.... Is Forever

Children

Children are your signposts that point to Truth. They live in each moment as Love. They remind us of that import lesson. Seeing the world and being alive fully can only be done through the eyes of a child. They are the dance of Life playing in itself. Kneel down in front of your child and view their world from their incredible height and laugh at what you see. (your Self)

Message for My Children

Stop and listen, what do you hear in the Silence..... your Self
The Silence is All
Live there and be That Silence
IT never ends and never begins just as you
It rides under the waves and is the waves just as you
It turns thoughts into open sky just as you
It allows love to flow just as you

Know IT in chaos
Know IT always
IT is the void you search for
IT is you
Rest into IT
Stop, be the stillness and the movement
Once you are the Void you are done
Now go and play

I Saw Him as a Wall

He was there between me and Peace
Blocking the time I felt I needed
The time for me, myself, my free time to recharge

My place was free, silent and me nothing but
I yearned to get there as a vacationer to the beach
Its owed to me and needed I would say
My batteries desire this refreshing

I saw him as a wall
He was only 5 years old
Telling me to stop and be Here
I moved through feeding pats of love like candy
Never really tasting the sweetness

I now see him as a wall
Holding me in, in Clarity
Holding me in Love

A Son

I watched my boy fly in the sky
Through rainstorms and thunder he would fly
Every once in a while in the corner of his eye
A tear would fall as he would try

Try to fit in
Try to catch something
Try to find his own way
Try all the things I once was

His tears will one day end his flight
Blur his vision and create new sight
And he will see at once his place to land
Right here where he took off from - where I stand

Mother

The bond between child and mother
Is the stream to the Ocean
It may wind to a trickle but it always moves
Towards its destination
Not Knowing it came from the Ocean
It goes onward to Home
Not Knowing it is Home now

My Children

My children are my teachers
Clouds of thunder dance through their minds
Shaking them as little trees
Supporting them I hold their Peace
Showing them that all thunder comes and goes
"Plant your roots deep my children and do not move"
"Look Real at the thunder and Peace is there"
"Look Real at the thunder and listen to your roar"

A Talk with a Son

Feel This
My arms around you
This is Real
This is Love
This is always Here
Feel This
My arms around you
It costs nothing
It never stops
It always makes you Feel - Good!
It always makes you feel Loved
With my arms around you - This is Love, This is Home, This is you.

PB&J

Spreading the jelly onto the bread
I am suddenly the jelly, the knife, the bread
There it is, me as It again, ahhh there is no me

Father

A river of wisdom runs down the mountain
Laughing and singing all the way down
This river laughs because it knows it is the Ocean
Enjoying the ride and sharing along the way
Sharing its joy, its connection

Wisdom is the silent lesson picked up by a child
No words
No language
Just knowing That
Just feeling That

This river of wisdom is Father
Always Here.

Stories

The Princess and the Alligator

Once upon a time there was a princess who lived near a river. This princess had a favorite dress she liked to wear. It was her finest dress and brought her lots of attention and happiness. The river served as the best way to clean her dress.

Each night the princess would go for a swim in the river when no one was watching to clean her dress from the days dirt. She loved how beautiful the dress looked and felt when she was done.

Deep in the woods by the river lived an alligator that tried to eat the princess every night as she came to and from the river. The princess spent all her days worrying about the alligator destroying her dress and devising ways to appease, go around, over and beyond the alligator. All these worries caused the princess to start carrying heavy rocks with her each night as she walked to the river to ward off the alligator.

Once night the princess was in the river cleaning her dress, when she got out of the river she snagged her dress on one of the rocks she brought with her. Seeing this the alligator took the opportunity to move in and do what alligators do. He chomped and ripped the dress off the princess and ate it whole.

Now the princess ran into the house naked and in terror. Thoughts raced through her mind, her life was over as she knew it, and she collapsed on the floor from all the drama. Minutes later she awoke and saw her Self in the mirror for the first time without her dress. Naked, beautiful and natural.

To this day the princess wears no dress and invites all her friends to wash their best dresses in her river.

Picture There

Once there was a little girl who loved to watch TV in her dads' car as he drove through the country.

Her favorite TV program was Country Roads.

It was about a car driving through a meadow.

The little girl loved this TV program, it made her feel peaceful.

"I wish I was there," she would say to her dad.

Unaware, her favorite program was a live video from the hood of the car.

Her TV program was the same car and same meadow she was in.

The little girl was so engrossed in her TV program that she failed to notice that she was already there.

If only she had turned off the TV and looked out the window.

A Happy Ending To the Story.

One day the TV broke.

The Flower

Once a flower bloomed on a beautiful spring morning and said,
"I wish I was part of nature"
Once the earth spun and rotated around the sun within the galaxy and said,
"I wish I was in space with all the other stars"
Once there was a little bird flying in the sky looking for the color blue
Once there was a dolphin riding the waves looking for the Sea
Once there was a man who yearned to be close to God

Story of a Girl

Once a girl thought she found Peace in her backyard
Her backyard was full of flowers and a pond
Peace appeared every time she sat in her yard

Her days were very stressed as she ran through them with one goal in mind
To get to her back yard to be in Peace

Each morning on her way to the market she would race past the dogwoods
Missing the birds singing the morning songs while the breezes flapped the leaves

Each afternoon she would run past the corn fields
And miss the Stillness that pulled the corn to new heights

And each late afternoon she would busily prepare dinner
And miss the taste within the flavor of each meal

And finally after dinner she would run to her backyard to rest into the Peace that she has
been all day.

The Servant and the Princess

A servant fell in love with a beautiful princess.
The two merged as One
No individuals, just Love

The mirror always reflects you

But like the Ying and Yang the servant felt sad
As he saw the opposite of oneness
Each night in dreams he was alone
As he drifted off to sleep beside his princess and into a dreamland where she was not included
Dark in separation
But upon awakening each morning he re connected with his Love as his nighttime illusion ended

The trees in the forest come from the same seed as the tree in the meadow

After a time the princess left the servant
Preyed by her own thoughts and reasons she left her Love
The servant was in agony over his lost love.
His days were long and lonely
But now his nights were bliss as he dreamed of their once romance

The Servant and the Princess (continued)

But only to find his mornings dark as he awoke alone

What you search for you are
Other is an illusion

Pain became too much in his days
So the servant started a path to find his lost love
Searching inward, outward everywhere
Like a bird trying to reach the sky
He searched new dreamlands journeying to new places
Like the scholar
He searched his mind and the minds of others
Like the shark hunting its prey
His hunger was never satisfied
After years of his pursuit the servant drove himself into madness and exhaustion and surrendered
In a state of pure surrender the servant gave up on his search for Love.

It was in that surrender that he rested into the Peace he sought and realized his Oneness that had never left him.

The Love you are is sitting in an Open Door

That night the servant met his Princess one more time
As she appeared and gave him a kiss in his dreams
And the servant knew his love was not the princess but all along the Self he sought.

Love packaged in another it is not
Love only here or there is not either
Love is you…. is another…. is Truth

Now the servant is Love in the day and Love in the night. He is no more a servant, a searcher, a seeker, he is only…. Love.

NOTES